Gift . Live Love,
Give Love and
Receive Love.

Nuff Love

2022 May 5

Love is a Battlefield

Halcourth Delando O'Gilvie

authorHOUSE®

AuthorHouse™
1663 Liberty Drive
Bloomington, IN 47403
www.authorhouse.com
Phone: 833-262-8899

Published by AuthorHouse 02/10/2021

ISBN: 978-1-6655-1687-7 (sc)
ISBN: 978-1-6655-1686-0 (hc)
ISBN: 978-1-6655-1685-3 (e)

Library of Congress Control Number: 2021902874

Contents

PRELUDE...ix

ACKNOWLEDGEMENTS...xi

BE MY VALENTINE PRECIOUS JESUS I PRAY.....................1

TIME AND LOVE...3

CAN I HAVE YOUR LOVE...5

BUT I KNOW THAT YOU LOVE ME BY THE SOUND OF
          YOUR HEART BEAT..7

FOREVER..9

MY HEART IS DRAWN TO YOU...11

PLEASE LET ME KNOW...13

MY HEART LEAPS...15

IN A MOMENT IN TIME...17

THE DOOR TO MY HEART IS OPEN FOR YOU..................19

A TRUE LOVE..21

I FOUND THE ONE MY HEART LOVES, MY KING..............23

I CAN FEEL YOUR PAIN MY SISTER...................................25

WILL YOU BE MY VALENTINE?...27

FROM YOUR POSITION UPON YOUR HOLY THRONE.......29

THERE IS NO HALF WAY WITH YOU PRECIOUS HOLY FATHER.......31

I WILL BE YOUR SWEET FRAGRANCE PRECIOUS JESUS.................33

TEACH ME HOW TO OPEN THE DOOR OF LOVE PRECIOUS
    HOLY SPIRIT 35

IN THE NICK OF TIME LOVE SAVED ME (The thief on the cross)........ 37

PLEASE REMEMBER ME 39

OUT OF YOUR HEART 41

I CAN SEE YOU 43

THAT SHE NEEDS..45

IF YOU SAY SO! 47

WHAT CAN I DO TO LET YOU KNOW THAT I LOVE YOU?..................49

I LOVE IT WHEN 51

I AM IN LOVE WITH YOU SWEET LADY 53

I AM GOING TO LOVE YOU FOREVER................................55

PLEASE BLESS HER PRECIOUS LORD JESUS I PRAY 57

MAKE JESUS YOUR FIRST LOVE....................................59

I LONG..61

PLEASE GIVE ME A LITTLE TIME 63

HAPPY NEW YEAR..65

TRUE LOVE..67

LIKE I CAN'T 69

WHEN I SAY I DO..71

PLEASE KEEP YOUR HEART FOR ME............................73

WHEN..75

IN YOU..77

YOUR LOVE SWEET LADY 79

THE BEST REVENGE IS NO REVENGE AT ALL 81

I GIVE MY HEART TO YOU...83

I AM ALWAYS HERE FOR YOU..85

FOR YOU...87

I WANT YOU BESIDE ME PRECIOUS JESUS............................89

MY LOVE FOR YOU..91

I CHOOSE YOU..93

NOT FOR LACK OF LOVE...95

ALL OF ME..97

IS THAT SOMEONE YOU?..99

YOU SAY YOU ARE OK BUT THAT IS NOT QUITE TRUE.......101

THIS IS WHY I LOVE YOU...103

ABOUT THE AUTHOR..105

PRELUDE

I say this without Hesitation and without Reservation, the Best Love ♥ you can have, is the LOVE OF JESUS CHRIST. The Best Lover you can have is someone who LOVES JESUS CHRIST.

LOVE should not be a roller coaster ride, but it is. There are eight types of LOVE according to the Ancient Greeks:

1. **Agape** — Unconditional Love. *"**Agape** is the highest form of love and it is the love of God for man and man for God."*

2. **Eros** — Romanic Love. *"**Eros** is named after the Greek god of love and fertility. It is a primal love that comes as a natural instinct for most people. It is a passionate love displayed through physical affection."*

3. **Philia** — Affectionate Love. *"**Philia** love is a close friendship or brotherly love."*

4. **Philautia** — Self Love. *"**Philautia** is essential for any relationship, we can only love others if we truly love ourselves and we can only care for others if we truly care for ourselves."* Love always starts within oneself before anything else.

5. **Storge** — Familiar Love. *"**Storge** or familiar love refers to the natural or instinctual affection such as the love of parent to a child."*

6. *Pragma* — Enduring Love. "*Pragma* is a unique bonded love that matures over many years. It's an everlasting love between a couple that chooses to put equal efforts into their relationship."
7. *Ludus* — Playful Love. "*Ludus* is a child-like and flirtatious love commonly found in the beginning stages of a relationship."
8. *Mania* — Obsessive Love. "*Mania* is an obsessive love towards a partner. It leads to unwanted jealousy or possessiveness."

But the LOVE I LOVE THE MOST is the LOVE OF PRECIOUS JESUS. HIS LOVE ♥ IS UNCONDITIONAL. You and I cannot buy His LOVE, You and I cannot earn His LOVE. HIS LOVE IS ALL YOU AND I NEED AND HIS LOVE IS ALL YOU AND I REQUIRE AND HIS LOVE IS ALL YOU AND I SHOULD DESIRE.

ACKNOWLEDGEMENTS

Special thanks to my sweet sister Chenieve O'Gilvie (aka my second mom) and also my charming wife, Joanne O'Gilvie (aka T-Guchi) for the Cover Image. Without your valuable input and unwavering dedication, this project would still be on the shelf. With my deepest appreciation, I pray Our Heavenly Father's Blessings to you both. Nuff Love Always.

Cover photo provided by Joanne O'Gilvie. Here is how the photo came about. "One day as I watched from the kitchen window, Hal was backing out of the garage and I noticed the heart shaped imprint left by the tire tracks on the driveway. I ran to get my camera to capture the moment, just in the nick of time, a few minutes later the image disappeared. Hal has attempted to replicate the double hearts but to no avail. It was and will forever be a memorable expression of love."

BE MY VALENTINE PRECIOUS JESUS I PRAY

BE MY VALENTINE PRECIOUS JESUS I PRAY. BECAUSE YOU HAVE LOVED ME SO ENDLESSLY IN MY SINFUL WAY.

BE MY VALENTINE PRECIOUS JESUS I PRAY. PLEASE OPEN MY HEART AND GRANT ME YOUR FAVOUR EVERY DAY.

BE MY VALENTINE PRECIOUS JESUS I PRAY. PLEASE BLESS ME WITH YOUR TREASURES AND ENVELOP ME WITH YOUR PLEASURES.

BE MY VALENTINE PRECIOUS JESUS I PRAY. PLEASE HELP ME TO KNOW HOW MUCH YOU CARE AND HOW MUCH YOU WANT TO SHARE.

BE MY VALENTINE PRECIOUS JESUS I PRAY. PLEASE HOLD MY HAND AND GENTLY LEAD ME IN YOUR ETERNAL PLAN.

BE MY VALENTINE PRECIOUS JESUS I PRAY. PLEASE TAKE AWAY ALL MY DOUBTS AND PLEASE TELL ME WHAT YOU ARE ALL ABOUT.

BE MY VALENTINE PRECIOUS JESUS I PRAY. PLEASE HELP ME TO APPRECIATE THE LOVE YOU GIVE THAT ALLOWS ME TO LIVE.

PRECIOUS JESUS, THIS IS MY APPRECIATION FOR THE PERFECT LOVE YOU HAVE LAVISHED ON ME. I THANK YOU PRECIOUS JESUS FOR YOUR UNFAILING LOVE. YOUR LOVE IS THE LOVE I DESIRE AND YOUR LOVE IS THE ONLY LOVE I REQUIRE. I THANK YOU FOR YOUR LOVE PRECIOUS JESUS. NOW AND ALWAYS. AMEN AND AMEN.

TIME AND LOVE

TIME AND LOVE WILL TAKE AWAY THE PAIN. TIME AND LOVE WILL MAKE YOU FALL IN LOVE ONCE AGAIN.

TIME AND LOVE WILL MAKE ALL THINGS NEW. TIME AND LOVE WILL MAKE THE GREY SKIES BLUE.

TIME AND LOVE WILL OPEN YOUR HEART. TIME AND LOVE WILL GIVE YOU A BRAND NEW START.

TIME AND LOVE IS THE CURE FOR ALL. TIME AND LOVE WILL HELP YOU WHEN YOU FALL.

TIME AND LOVE WILL TAKE AWAY ALL YOUR TEARS. TIME AND LOVE WILL SHOW HOW MUCH THE ONE WHO LOVES YOU CARES.

TIME AND LOVE WILL MAKE YOU STRONG. TIME AND LOVE WILL TAKE AWAY ALL THAT'S WRONG.

TIME AND LOVE WILL GIVE YOU HOPE. TIME AND LOVE WILL HELP YOU COPE.

LOVE IS A BEAUTIFUL THING SWEET LADY. WHEN YOU TRULY LOVE SOMEONE, YOU WANT THE BEST FOR HIM OR HER. I TRULY LOVE YOU SWEET LADY AND I PRAY OUR HEAVENLY FATHER GIVES YOU THE BEST. NUFF LOVE ALWAYS.

CAN I HAVE YOUR LOVE

CAN I HAVE YOUR LOVE EVERY SECOND OF EVERY MINUTE. CAN I HAVE YOUR LOVE AND ALL THE SWEETNESS THAT IS WITHIN IT.

CAN I HAVE YOUR LOVE EVERY MINUTE OF EVERY HOUR. CAN I HAVE YOUR LOVE WITH ALL YOUR GOODNESS AND ALL YOUR POWER.

CAN I HAVE YOUR LOVE EVERY HOUR OF EVERY DAY. CAN I HAVE YOUR LOVE, PLEASE GIVE IT TO ME IS WHAT I PRAY.

CAN I HAVE YOUR LOVE EVERY DAY OF EVERY WEEK. CAN I HAVE YOUR LOVE, YOUR LOVE ONLY WILL I SEEK.

CAN I HAVE YOUR LOVE EVERY WEEK OF EVERY MONTH. CAN I HAVE YOUR LOVE, SWEET LADY YOU ARE PRECIOUS TO LOOK AT FROM BEHIND AND IN FRONT.

CAN I HAVE YOUR LOVE EVERY MONTH OF EVERY YEAR. CAN I HAVE YOUR LOVE, SWEET LADY I WILL SHOW YOU HOW MUCH I CARE.

CAN I HAVE YOUR LOVE EVERY YEAR THAT WE LIVE. CAN I HAVE YOUR LOVE AND MY LOVE TO YOU I WILL GIVE.

I WAS JUST DRIVING ALONG TODAY AND YOU ENTERED MY THOUGHTS AND I CAME UP WITH THESE WORDS. GOD BLESS YOU NOW AND ALWAYS SWEET LADY. AMEN AND AMEN.

BUT I KNOW THAT YOU LOVE ME BY THE SOUND OF YOUR HEART BEAT

YOU DON'T ALWAYS SAY IN WORDS THAT YOU LOVE ME. BUT I KNOW THAT YOU LOVE ME BY THE SOUND OF YOUR HEART BEAT.

WHEN I LOOK INTO YOUR EYES, THEY SEND ME A MESSAGE. BUT I KNOW THAT YOU LOVE ME BY THE SOUND OF YOUR HEART BEAT.

WHEN I HOLD YOUR HAND, I CAN FEEL IT IN YOUR TOUCH. BUT I KNOW THAT YOU LOVE ME BY THE SOUND OF YOUR HEART BEAT.

WHEN I WALK WITH YOU ALONG THE WAY, I FEEL HAPPY AND BRIGHT, ALL THROUGHOUT THE DAY. BUT I KNOW THAT YOU LOVE ME BY THE SOUND OF YOUR HEART BEAT.

WHEN YOU SMILE AT ME, I KNOW FOR SURE. BUT I KNOW THAT YOU LOVE ME BY THE SOUND OF YOUR HEART BEAT.

WHEN YOU KISS ME, I FEEL IT UPON YOUR LIPS. BUT I KNOW THAT YOU LOVE ME BY THE SOUND OF YOUR HEART BEAT.

WHEN YOU SAY YOU LOVE ME THAT I KNOW FOR SURE. BUT I KNOW THAT YOU LOVE ME BY THE SOUND OF YOUR HEART BEAT.

SWEET LADY, I KNOW THAT YOU LOVE ME BY THE SOUND OF YOUR HEART BEAT. JUST SO YOU KNOW, I LOVE TO HEAR THE SOUND OF YOUR HEART BEAT. GOD BLESS YOU ALWAYS.

FOREVER

I DON'T WANT TO HOLD YOUR HAND, UNLESS I CAN HOLD YOUR HAND FOREVER.

I DON'T WANT TO WALK BESIDE YOU, UNLESS I CAN WALK BESIDE YOU FOREVER.

I DON'T WANT TO TALK TO YOU, UNLESS I CAN TALK TO YOU FOREVER.

I DON'T WANT TO DINE WITH YOU, UNLESS I CAN DINE WITH YOU FOREVER.

I DON'T WANT TO SMILE WITH YOU, UNLESS I CAN SMILE WITH YOU FOREVER.

I DON'T WANT TO PRAY WITH YOU, UNLESS I CAN PRAY WITH YOU FOREVER.

I DON'T WANT TO LOVE YOU, UNLESS I CAN LOVE YOU FOREVER.

IT IS SO EASY TO DO ALL THESE THINGS WITH SOMEONE. BUT I AM LETTING YOU KNOW, IF IT IS NOT FOREVER WITH YOU, I DON'T WANT TO DO IT AT ALL. MY HEART IS YOURS FOREVER, IF YOU WANT IT. GOD BLESS YOU ALWAYS.

MY HEART IS DRAWN TO YOU

THERE IS A SWEETNESS IN YOU THAT I ADORE, I SENSED IT WHEN I FIRST WALKED THROUGH YOUR HEART'S DOOR. I CAN TRULY SAY, MY HEART IS DRAWN TO YOU.

THERE IS A GENTLENESS IN YOU I SEE, I SENSED IT WHEN YOU FIRST LOOKED AT ME. I CAN TRULY SAY, MY HEART IS DRAWN TO YOU.

THERE IS A MEEKNESS IN YOU THAT I LOVE, I KNOW IT WAS GIVEN TO YOU FROM OUR FATHER UP ABOVE. I CAN TRULY SAY, MY HEART IS DRAWN TO YOU.

THERE IS A KINDNESS IN YOU THAT I LIKE, YOU ARE WILLING TO FORGIVE RATHER THAN PUT UP A FIGHT. I CAN TRULY SAY, MY HEART IS DRAWN TO YOU.

THERE IS A GOODNESS IN YOU THAT I ADMIRE, I HOPE THE SPIRIT OF THE LORD WILL GIVE YOU ALL THAT YOU DESIRE. I CAN TRULY SAY, MY HEART IS DRAWN TO YOU.

THERE IS A COURAGE IN YOU THAT I SEE, I PRAY THAT COURAGE COULD BECOME A PART OF ME. I CAN TRULY SAY, MY HEART IS DRAWN TO YOU.

THERE IS A LOVE IN YOU THAT I WILL CHERISH, I PRAY TO OUR HEAVENLY FATHER ABOVE THAT LOVE WILL NEVER PERISH. I CAN TRULY SAY, MY HEART IS DRAWN TO YOU.

THESE ARE THE THOUGHTS THAT COME TO ME WHEN I THINK ABOUT YOU. I HOPE AND PRAY THAT OUR HEAVENLY FATHER WILL RICHLY BLESS YOU NOW AND ALWAYS. AMEN AND AMEN.

PLEASE LET ME KNOW

IS THERE SOMETHING YOU WANT TO TELL ME, PLEASE LET ME KNOW. IS THERE SOMETHING YOU WANT TO TELL ME, I WON'T STAND IN YOUR WAY IF YOU HAVE TO GO, PLEASE LET ME KNOW.

IS THERE SOMETHING ON YOUR MIND, PLEASE LET ME KNOW. IS THERE SOMETHING ON YOUR MIND, PLEASE DON'T BE AFRAID TO LET ME KNOW.

IS THERE SOMETHING YOU WANT TO SAY, PLEASE LET ME KNOW, IS THERE SOMETHING YOU WANT TO SAY, I WILL UNDERSTAND IF YOU HAVE TO GO, PLEASE LET ME KNOW.

IS THERE SOMETHING YOU HAVE TO DO, PLEASE LET ME KNOW, IS THERE SOMETHING I CAN HELP YOU THROUGH, PLEASE LET ME KNOW.

IS THERE SOMETHING YOU CAN'T HANDLE, PLEASE LET ME KNOW, IS THERE SOMETHING YOU CAN'T HANDLE I WILL UNDERSTAND IF YOU HAVE TO GO, PLEASE LET ME KNOW.

IS THERE SOMETHING YOU HAVE LOST HOPE WITH, PLEASE LET ME KNOW, IS THERE SOMETHING YOU CAN'T COPE WITH, PLEASE LET ME KNOW.

IS THERE SOMETHING WE CAN'T OVERCOME, PLEASE LET ME KNOW.
IS THERE SOMETHING WE CAN'T OVERCOME, I WILL UNDERSTAND
IF YOU HAVE TO LET GO, PLEASE LET ME KNOW.

PLEASE UNDERSTAND THAT I TRULY TREASURE YOU. YOU ARE
THOUGHTFUL, CARING AND GENEROUS AND THAT IS WHAT I AM
LOOKING FOR. PLEASE ENVELOP YOURSELF IN THE PRECIOUS ARMS
OF JESUS. THERE IS ALWAYS HOPE. GOD BLESS YOU ALWAYS.

MY HEART LEAPS

MY HEART LEAPS WHEN I THINK OF OUR POTENTIAL.

MY HEART LEAPS WHEN I THINK OF OUR ACCOMPLISHMENTS.

MY HEART LEAPS WHEN I THINK OF OUR UNITY.

MY HEART LEAPS WHEN I THINK OF OUR HISTORY.

MY HEART LEAPS WHEN I THINK OF OUR HOPE.

MY HEART LEAPS WHEN I THINK OF OUR FUTURE.

MY HEART LEAPS WHEN I THINK OF OUR LOVE.

NOTHING BEATS TRUE LOVE. TRUE LOVE IS PATIENT AND TRUE
LOVE IS UNDERSTANDING. IT MAKES NO SENSE TO HURRY LOVE.
TRUE LOVE COMES WHEN WE LEAST EXPECT IT. TRUE LOVE IS
ALWAYS KIND, TRUE LOVE IS YOU OH SPECIAL FRIEND OF MINE.
NUFF LOVE ALWAYS.

IN A MOMENT IN TIME

IN A MOMENT IN TIME, WE WILL EMBRACE. IN A MOMENT IN TIME, WE WILL MEET FACE TO FACE.

IN A MOMENT IN TIME, WE WILL LOVE. IN A MOMENT IN TIME, WE WILL BE BLESSED FROM ABOVE.

IN A MOMENT IN TIME, WE WILL HOLD HANDS. IN A MOMENT IN TIME, WE WILL MAKE OUR PLANS.

IN A MOMENT IN TIME, WE WILL WALK TOGETHER. IN A MOMENT IN TIME, WE WILL LIVE FOREVER.

IN A MOMENT IN TIME, WE WILL HOLD EACH OTHER. IN A MOMENT IN TIME, WE WILL BE SORRY NEVER.

IN A MOMENT IN TIME, WE WILL KISS AGAIN. IN A MOMENT IN TIME, WE WILL BE IN A PLACE WHERE TIME HAS NO END.

IN A MOMENT IN TIME, WE WILL EMBRACE. IN A MOMENT IN TIME, WE WILL HAVE ENDURED THIS CHALLENGING RACE.

AT TIMES OUR LIVES MAY SEEM DIFFICULT WITH A LOT OF OBSTACLES TO CLEAR. BUT AT ANY MOMENT IN TIME, THE DIFFICULT ROAD MAY TURN INTO PASTURES GREEN. WE HAVE TO CHERISH EACH MOMENT IN TIME.

THE DOOR TO MY HEART IS OPEN FOR YOU

THE DOOR TO MY HEART IS OPEN FOR YOU, PLEASE COME ON IN AND LET OUR CONVERSATION BEGIN.

THE DOOR TO MY HEART IS OPEN FOR YOU, YOU ARE WELCOME ANYTIME BECAUSE YOU ARE A PRECIOUS FRIEND OF MINE.

THE DOOR TO MY HEART IS OPEN FOR YOU, PLEASE MAKE YOURSELF AT HOME, THERE IS NO MORE NEED FOR YOU TO ROAM.

THE DOOR TO MY HEART IS OPEN FOR YOU, YOU ARE PRECIOUS TO ME BECAUSE YOU HAVE PRECIOUS JESUS BEAUTY FOR ALL TO SEE.

THE DOOR TO MY HEART IS OPEN FOR YOU, PLEASE FEEL FREE TO MOVE AROUND BECAUSE ONE DAY YOU WILL BE WEARING THE MOST BEAUTIFUL WHITE WEDDING GOWN.

THE DOOR TO MY HEART IS OPEN FOR YOU, YOU ARE ALWAYS WELCOME HERE BECAUSE FOR YOU I WILL ALWAYS CARE.

THE DOOR TO MY HEART IS OPEN FOR YOU, PLEASE DON'T HESITATE TO TAKE A REST BECAUSE FOR YOU I WILL ALWAYS DO MY BEST.

THE GOOD WORD SAYS "ABOVE ALL THINGS PROTECT YOUR HEART BECAUSE OUT OF IT FLOWS THE ISSUES OF LIFE", PARAPHRASING PROVERBS 4:23. THE DOOR TO MY HEART IS ALWAYS OPEN FOR YOU. GOD BLESS YOU ALWAYS.

A TRUE LOVE

ALL I WANT IS A TRUE LOVE, JUST MY BEST FRIEND TO BE WITH ME WHERE TIME NEVER ENDS.

ALL I WANT IS A TRUE LOVE, SOMEONE TO HOLD MY HAND TO HELP ME WITH OUR FATHER'S ETERNAL PLAN.

ALL I WANT IS A TRUE LOVE, A SPECIAL KIND OF LADY, NO ONE SLY, NO ONE SHADY.

ALL I WANT IS A TRUE LOVE, SOMEONE TO WALK WITH ME ALONG THE WAY INTO ETERNITY.

ALL I WANT IS A TRUE LOVE, A SWEET GIRL WHO WILL ALWAYS TAKE ME FOR A TWIRL.

ALL I WANT IS A TRUE LOVE, SOMEONE WHO WILL ALWAYS HOLD ME TIGHT AND SQUEEZE ME GENTLY THROUGHOUT THE NIGHT.

ALL I WANT IS A TRUE LOVE, THAT SPECIAL SOMEONE WHO WOULD FOREVER BE THE ONLY ONE.

TRUE LOVE IS PATIENT AND TRUE LOVE IS KIND, TRUE LOVE IS NEVER HASTY AND TRUE LOVE IS NEVER UNKIND. WHEN WE FIND THAT ONE TRUE LOVE, PLEASE, PLEASE DO WHAT IT TAKES TO MAKE IT LAST FOREVER.

I FOUND THE ONE MY HEART LOVES, MY KING

I FOUND THE ONE MY HEART LOVES. HE TREATS ME LIKE A QUEEN, BETTER THAN ANY MOVIE SCENE.

I FOUND THE ONE MY HEART LOVES. HE HOLDS ME CLOSE AND TELLS ME HE LOVES ME THE MOST.

I FOUND THE ONE MY HEART LOVES. HE SHOWS ME KINDNESS AND HAS TAKEN AWAY ALL MY BLINDNESS.

I FOUND THE ONE MY HEART LOVES. HE BRIGHTENS MY DAYS AS WE WALK ALONG IN THE SUN'S RAYS.

I FOUND THE ONE MY HEART LOVES. HE GIVES ME HOPE AND HE HAS BROADENED MY SCOPE.

I FOUND THE ONE MY HEART LOVES. HE GIVES ME PLEASURE THAT I WILL ALWAYS TREASURE.

I FOUND THE ONE MY HEART LOVES. HE MAKES ME COMPLETE, HE MAKES ME FEEL NEAT, HE MAKES ME FEEL EVER SO SWEET.

IN YOU, I HAVE FOUND THE ONE I LOVE. MY HEART IS AT EASE AND I AM WELL PLEASED. I WILL ALWAYS GIVE MY LOVE TO YOU BECAUSE IN YOU I HAVE FOUND THE ONE I LOVE.

I CAN FEEL YOUR PAIN MY SISTER

I CAN FEEL YOUR PAIN MY SISTER BUT I DON'T KNOW WHAT TO DO. I CAN FEEL YOUR PAIN MY SISTER, I HAVE TO ASK MY PRECIOUS JESUS WHAT TO DO.

I CAN FEEL YOUR PAIN MY SISTER, I CAN FEEL IT SO MUCH. I CAN FEEL YOUR PAIN MY SISTER, I WILL ASK MY PRECIOUS JESUS TO REACH OUT HIS HAND AND TOUCH.

I CAN FEEL YOUR PAIN MY SISTER, IT IS MORE THAN I CAN BEAR. I CAN FEEL YOUR PAIN MY SISTER, I WILL ASK PRECIOUS JESUS TO STAY BESIDE YOU BECAUSE HE REALLY CARES.

I CAN FEEL YOUR PAIN MY SISTER, IT HURTS ME TO SEE YOU THIS WAY. I CAN FEEL YOUR PAIN MY SISTER, I WILL LET PRECIOUS JESUS TAKE OVER BECAUSE FOR YOU A PRICE HE DID PAY.

I CAN FEEL YOUR PAIN MY SISTER, I WILL BE SILENT WHILE YOU TALK. I CAN FEEL YOUR PAIN MY SISTER, WITH MY PRECIOUS JESUS I WILL SEND YOU FOR A WALK.

I CAN FEEL YOUR PAIN MY SISTER AND I PROMISE I WILL GET DOWN ON MY KNEES AND PRAY. I CAN FEEL YOUR PAIN MY

SISTER, I WILL HAVE TO DO THIS WITH MY PRECIOUS JESUS EACH AND EVERY DAY.

I CAN FEEL YOUR PAIN MY SISTER BUT I KNOW YOU WILL BE SET FREE. I CAN FEEL YOUR PAIN MY SISTER BUT I HAVE TO TELL YOU, MY PRECIOUS JESUS PROMISED HE WILL ALWAYS BE THERE FOR THEE.

MY SISTER, PUT YOUR FAITH, YOUR HOPES, YOUR DREAMS AND YOUR PAIN IN THE PRECIOUS ARMS OF JESUS. PRECIOUS JESUS HAS PROMISED THAT HE WILL NEVER LEAVE YOU NOR WILL HE FORSAKE YOU. IF YOU CAN'T COUNT ON ANYONE ELSE, YOU CAN COUNT ON HIM. GOD BLESS YOU MY SISTER NOW AND ALWAYS. AMEN AND AMEN.

WILL YOU BE MY VALENTINE?

EVERY SECOND OF EVERY MINUTE, I WILL ASK, WILL YOU BE MY VALENTINE?

EVERY MINUTE OF EVERY HOUR, I WILL ASK, WILL YOU BE MY VALENTINE?

EVERY HOUR OF EVERY DAY, I WILL ASK, WILL YOU BE MY VALENTINE?

EVERY DAY OF EVERY WEEK, I WILL ASK, WILL YOU BE MY VALENTINE?

EVERY WEEK OF EVERY MONTH, I WILL ASK, WILL YOU BE MY VALENTINE?

EVERY MONTH OF EVERY YEAR, I WILL ASK, WILL YOU BE MY VALENTINE?

I HOPE ONE DAY YOU WILL SAY, YOU WILL ALWAYS BE MY VALENTINE.

GOD BLESS YOU. I HOPE AND PRAY FOR YOU ALL OF OUR HEAVENLY FATHER'S RICH AND WONDERFUL BLESSINGS, NOW AND ALWAYS. NUFF LOVE.

FROM YOUR POSITION UPON YOUR HOLY THRONE

FROM YOUR POSITION UPON YOUR HOLY THRONE, PLEASE SEND YOUR LOVE TO YOUR VERY OWN, PRECIOUS HOLY FATHER I PRAY.

FROM YOUR POSITION UPON YOUR HOLY THRONE, PLEASE SEND YOUR WEALTH AND PROSPERITY TO YOUR VERY OWN, PRECIOUS HOLY FATHER I PRAY.

FROM YOUR POSITION UPON YOUR HOLY THRONE, PLEASE SEND YOUR BLESSINGS TO YOUR VERY OWN, PRECIOUS HOLY FATHER I PRAY.

FROM YOUR POSITION UPON YOUR HOLY THRONE, PLEASE SEND YOUR PROTECTION TO YOUR VERY OWN, PRECIOUS HOLY FATHER I PRAY.

FROM YOUR POSITION UPON YOUR HOLY THRONE, PLEASE SEND YOUR HONOUR TO YOUR VERY OWN, PRECIOUS HOLY FATHER I PRAY.

FROM YOUR POSITION UPON YOUR HOLY THRONE, PLEASE SEND YOUR GRACE TO YOUR VERY OWN, PRECIOUS HOLY FATHER I PRAY.

FROM YOUR POSITION UPON YOUR HOLY THRONE, PLEASE SEND YOUR MERCIES TO YOUR VERY OWN, PRECIOUS HOLY FATHER I PRAY.

PRECIOUS HOLY FATHER, YOU SEE ALL OUR FRAILTIES, YOU SEE ALL OUR WANTS, YOU SEE ALL OUR NEEDS AND YOU SEE ALL OUR DESIRES. PLEASE SEND DOWN YOUR BOUNTIFUL BLESSINGS UPON US PRECIOUS HOLY FATHER I PRAY. I ASK THIS IN THE PRECIOUS NAME OF JESUS. AMEN AND AMEN.

PSALM 31:19 (NIV) *How abundant are the good things that you have stored up for those who fear you, that you bestow in the sight of all, on those who take refuge in you.*

THERE IS NO HALF WAY WITH YOU PRECIOUS HOLY FATHER

THERE IS NO HALF WAY WITH YOU PRECIOUS HOLY FATHER, YOU PROVIDE YOUR LOVE FULLY.

THERE IS NO HALF WAY WITH YOU PRECIOUS HOLY FATHER, YOU PROVIDE YOUR GRACE FULLY.

THERE IS NO HALF WAY WITH YOU PRECIOUS HOLY FATHER, YOU PROVIDE YOUR MERCIES FULLY.

THERE IS NO HALF WAY WITH YOU PRECIOUS HOLY FATHER, YOU PROVIDE YOUR DAILY BREATH FULLY.

THERE IS NO HALF WAY WITH YOU PRECIOUS HOLY FATHER, YOU PROVIDE YOUR GOODNESS FULLY.

THERE IS NO HALF WAY WITH YOU PRECIOUS HOLY FATHER, YOU PROVIDE YOUR HOLY SPIRIT FULLY.

I THANK YOU HEAVENLY FATHER THAT THERE IS NO HALF-FINISHED BUSINESS WITH YOU. YOU PROVIDE FOR ALL YOUR CREATION YOUR FULNESS OF JOY IN THE PRECIOUS NAME OF JESUS. PLEASE TEACH US PRECIOUS HOLY SPIRIT HOW TO GIVE OUR FULNESS TO OUR HEAVENLY FATHER. IN JESUS MOST PRECIOUS NAME I PRAY. AMEN AND AMEN.

I WILL BE YOUR SWEET FRAGRANCE PRECIOUS JESUS

IN THIS WORLD THAT IS FILLED WITH GUILT AND FILTH, I WILL BE YOUR SWEET FRAGRANCE PRECIOUS JESUS.

IN AN AGE WHERE THERE IS ANGER AND RAGE, I WILL BE YOUR SWEET FRAGRANCE PRECIOUS JESUS.

IN THIS WORLD WHERE THERE IS SORROW AND HORROR, I WILL BE YOUR SWEET FRAGRANCE PRECIOUS JESUS.

IN AN AGE WHERE THERE IS DRAMA AND TRAUMA, I WILL BE YOUR SWEET FRAGRANCE PRECIOUS JESUS.

IN THIS WORLD WHERE THERE IS TROUBLE ON THE DOUBLE, I WILL BE YOUR SWEET FRAGRANCE PRECIOUS JESUS.

IN AN AGE WHERE THERE IS WORRY AND WE ARE ALWAYS IN A HURRY, I WILL BE YOUR SWEET FRAGRANCE PRECIOUS JESUS.

IN THIS WORLD WHERE THERE IS PAIN AND STRAIN, I WILL BE YOUR SWEET FRAGRANCE PRECIOUS JESUS.

PRECIOUS JESUS I WILL BE YOUR FLOWER THAT BLOOMS AND BECOME YOUR SWEET FRAGRANCE IN THIS WORLD. I WILL GIVE YOU ALL OF MY PRAISE AND ALL OF MY WORSHIP, NOW AND ALWAYS. AMEN AND AMEN.

TEACH ME HOW TO OPEN THE DOOR OF LOVE PRECIOUS HOLY SPIRIT

TEACH ME HOW TO OPEN THE DOOR OF LOVE PRECIOUS HOLY SPIRIT. PLEASE TEACH ME WHAT TO DO AND HOW TO DEPEND ONLY ON YOU.

TEACH ME HOW TO OPEN THE DOOR OF LOVE PRECIOUS HOLY SPIRIT. PLEASE TEACH ME HOW TO SOAR AND REMIND ME OF THE THINGS THAT YOU ADORE.

TEACH ME HOW TO OPEN THE DOOR OF LOVE PRECIOUS HOLY SPIRIT. PLEASE TEACH ME HOW TO LOVE AND TO FOCUS ON THE THINGS FROM HEAVEN ABOVE.

TEACH ME HOW TO OPEN THE DOOR OF LOVE PRECIOUS HOLY SPIRIT. PLEASE TEACH ME HOW TO SHARE BECAUSE I KNOW HOW MUCH YOU CARE.

TEACH ME HOW TO OPEN THE DOOR OF LOVE PRECIOUS HOLY SPIRIT. PLEASE TEACH ME HOW TO BE STILL AS I DO THY ETERNAL WILL.

TEACH ME HOW TO OPEN THE DOOR OF LOVE PRECIOUS HOLY SPIRIT. PLEASE TEACH ME HOW TO PRAISE AS I TURN MY EYES UPON YOU AND GAZE.

TEACH ME HOW TO OPEN THE DOOR OF LOVE PRECIOUS HOLY SPIRIT. PLEASE TEACH ME HOW TO PRAY AS I GO FROM DAY TO DAY.

I THANK YOU PRECIOUS HOLY SPIRIT FOR OPENING THE DOOR OF LOVE FOR ME. IN YOU PRECIOUS HOLY SPIRIT, I CAN HOPE FOR ALL THINGS THAT GLORIFY MY HEAVENLY FATHER. I GIVE YOU THANKS PRECIOUS HOLY SPIRIT IN THE MIGHTY NAME OF JESUS. AMEN AND AMEN.

IN THE NICK OF TIME LOVE SAVED ME (The thief on the cross)

I WAS HOPELESS AND LOST BUT IN THE NICK OF TIME PRECIOUS JESUS PAID THE COST. IN THE NICK OF TIME LOVE SAVED ME (The thief on the cross).

I WAS DESTINED TO DIE AND I DON'T THINK ANYONE WOULD DARE TO CRY. IN THE NICK OF TIME LOVE SAVED ME (The thief on the cross).

I WAS MARRED IN SIN AND I FELT GUILTY FROM WITHIN. IN THE NICK OF TIME LOVE SAVED ME (The thief on the cross).

I WAS HELLBOUND AND BY MY SAVIOUR I WAS FOUND. IN THE NICK OF TIME LOVE SAVED ME (The thief on the cross).

I HAD NO EXCUSE TO MAKE BUT PRECIOUS JESUS GRACE I DID TAKE. IN THE NICK OF TIME LOVE SAVED ME (The thief on the cross).

NOW I LIVE ON IN HISTORY AS ONE OF PRECIOUS JESUS GREAT MYSTERY. IN THE NICK OF TIME LOVE SAVED ME (The thief on the cross).

I WILL FOREVER TELL OF PRECIOUS JESUS LOVE AND HIS ETERNAL GRACE THAT FLOWS FROM HEAVEN UP ABOVE. IN THE NICK OF TIME LOVE SAVED ME (The thief on the cross).

I THANK YOU PRECIOUS JESUS THAT UPON THE CROSS YOUR ACT OF GRACE AND MERCY TOWARDS THE THIEF ON THE CROSS SHOWS HOW MUCH YOU LOVE US. I THANK YOU FOR YOUR ETERNAL LOVE FROM HEAVEN ABOVE AND I THANK YOU THAT IN THE NICK OF TIME YOU SAVED ME. I GIVE YOU ALL OF MY PRAISE AND ALL OF MY WORSHIP TO YOU PRECIOUS JESUS NOW AND FOREVERMORE. AMEN AND AMEN.

PLEASE REMEMBER ME

PLEASE REMEMBER ME WHO YOU DID CREATE WITHOUT BLEMISH, BUT SIN CREPT IN AND YOUR PRESENCE DIMINISHED. PLEASE REMEMBER ME PRECIOUS JESUS I PRAY.

PLEASE REMEMBER ME WHOM YOU HAVE REDEEMED WITH YOUR LIFE, HELP ME TO CHERISH YOU WITHOUT FUSS AND WITHOUT STRIFE. PLEASE REMEMBER ME PRECIOUS JESUS I PRAY.

PLEASE REMEMBER ME WHO SPURNED YOUR GRACE, BUT PLEASE REMEMBER ME BECAUSE I LONG FOR YOUR EMBRACE. PLEASE REMEMBER ME PRECIOUS JESUS I PRAY.

PLEASE REMEMBER ME AND SHOW ME YOUR MERCY AND PLEASE REMEMBER BECAUSE FOR YOU ONLY, MY SOUL IS SO THIRSTY. PLEASE REMEMBER ME PRECIOUS JESUS I PRAY.

PLEASE REMEMBER ME WHILE YOU HOLD ME IN YOUR ARMS, PLEASE REMEMBER ME WHILE I BASK IN ALL OF YOUR CHARMS. PLEASE REMEMBER ME PRECIOUS JESUS I PRAY.

PLEASE REMEMBER ME BECAUSE I AM RUNNING OUT OF TIME, PRECIOUS JESUS PLEASE REMEMBER ME SO I CAN LIVE WITH YOU SUBLIME. PLEASE REMEMBER ME PRECIOUS JESUS I PRAY.

PLEASE REMEMBER ME MY MERCIFUL MASTER, I THANK YOU FOR REMEMBERING ME AND RESCUING ME FROM ETERNAL DISASTER. THANK YOU FOR REMEMBERING ME PRECIOUS JESUS I PRAY.

PRECIOUS JESUS IS THERE ANY GOD LIKE YOU? YOU WILL GO TO THE UTTERMOST AND SAVE YOUR PEOPLE WITH THE POWER OF YOUR PRECIOUS HOLY GHOST. PRECIOUS JESUS THAT IS WHO YOU ARE. PRECIOUS JESUS, I GIVE YOU ALL OF MY PRAISE AND ALL OF MY WORSHIP NOW AND ALWAYS. AMEN AND AMEN.

OUT OF YOUR HEART

OUT OF YOUR HEART COMES LOVE AND OUT OF YOUR HEART COMES HATE. I HOPE THE LOVE OF PRECIOUS JESUS POURS OUT OF YOUR HEART AND I PRAY THAT LOVE WILL NEVER EVER DEPART.

OUT OF YOUR HEART COMES GOOD AND OUT OF YOUR HEART COMES EVIL. I HOPE THE GOODNESS OF PRECIOUS JESUS POURS OUT OF YOUR HEART AND I PRAY THAT GOODNESS WILL NEVER EVER DEPART.

OUT OF YOUR HEART COMES FAITH AND OUT OF YOUR HEART COMES FEAR. I HOPE THE FAITH OF PRECIOUS JESUS POURS OUT OF YOUR HEART AND I PRAY THAT FAITH WILL NEVER EVER DEPART.

OUT OF YOUR HEART COMES PEACE AND OUT OF YOUR HEART COMES WAR. I HOPE THE PEACE OF PRECIOUS JESUS POURS OUT OF YOUR HEART AND I PRAY THAT PEACE WILL NEVER EVER DEPART.

OUT OF YOUR HEART COMES JOY AND OUT OF YOUR HEART COMES SADNESS. I HOPE THE JOY OF PRECIOUS JESUS POURS

OUT OF YOUR HEART AND I PRAY THAT JOY WILL NEVER EVER DEPART.

OUT OF YOUR HEART COMES LAUGHTER AND OUT OF YOUR HEART COMES PAIN. I HOPE THE LAUGHTER OF PRECIOUS JESUS POURS OUT OF YOUR HEART AND I PRAY THAT LAUGHTER WILL NEVER EVER DEPART.

OUT OF YOUR HEART COMES LIGHT AND OUT OF YOUR HEART COMES DARKNESS. I HOPE THE LIGHT OF PRECIOUS JESUS POURS OUT OF YOUR HEART AND I PRAY THAT LIGHT WILL NEVER EVER DEPART.

PRECIOUS JESUS PLEASE LET YOUR LOVE, YOUR GOODNESS, YOUR FAITH, YOUR PEACE, YOUR JOY, YOUR LAUGHTER AND YOUR LIGHT POUR OUT OF MY HEART AND PLEASE HELP ME TO NEVER EVER LET IT DEPART. AMEN AND AMEN.

I CAN SEE YOU

I CAN SEE YOUR BEAUTIFUL FACE AND I CAN FEEL YOUR WARM EMBRACE.

I CAN SEE YOUR BEAUTIFUL SMILE AND IT SATISFIES ME MILE AFTER MILE.

I CAN SEE YOU CARESSING ME, SWEET LADY I WILL CHERISH YOU ENDLESSLY.

I CAN SEE YOU HOLDING ME CLOSE AS I WHISPER IN YOUR EAR, I LOVE YOU THE MOST.

I CAN SEE YOU HOLDING MY HAND, SWEET LADY I AM ASKING YOU WHAT IS OUR FUTURE PLAN?

I CAN SEE YOU WRAPPED IN MY ARMS AS I ENVELOP YOU WITH ALL OF MY CHARMS.

I CAN SEE YOU LOVING ME AND BY THE GRACE OF OUR HEAVENLY FATHER, I CAN SHOW YOU HOW TRUE LOVE SHOULD BE.

TRUE LOVE IS A BEAUTIFUL GIFT. IT ALLOWS YOUR HEART TO BE SET FREE. TRUE LOVE ALLOWS TWO HEARTS TO BE SET AT LIBERTY. GOD BLESS YOU ALWAYS.

THAT SHE NEEDS

PRECIOUS HOLY SPIRIT PLEASE LOVE HER AND GIVE HER THE EVERLASTING LOVE THAT SHE NEEDS.

PRECIOUS HOLY SPIRIT PLEASE BLESS HER AND GIVE HER THE EVERLASTING BLESSINGS THAT SHE NEEDS.

PRECIOUS HOLY SPIRIT PLEASE HOLD HER AND GIVE HER THE EVERLASTING SUPPORT THAT SHE NEEDS.

PRECIOUS HOLY SPIRIT PLEASE COMFORT HER AND GIVE HER THE EVERLASTING COMFORT THAT SHE NEEDS.

PRECIOUS HOLY SPIRIT PLEASE STRENGTHEN HER AND GIVE HER THE EVERLASTING STRENGTH THAT SHE NEEDS.

PRECIOUS HOLY SPIRIT PLEASE ENLARGE HER TERRITORIES AND GIVE HER YOUR EVERLASTING TERRITORIES THAT SHE NEEDS.

PRECIOUS HOLY SPIRIT PLEASE GIVE HER VISION AND GIVE HER THE EVERLASTING VISION THAT SHE NEEDS.

I THINK ABOUT YOU OFTEN YOUNG LADY AND THESE ARE THE THOUGHTS THAT ENTERS MY MIND. I WANT YOU TO KNOW THAT MY MIND IS MADE UP AND I WILL NOT HURT YOU. I PRAY OUR HEAVENLY FATHER'S RICH AND ETERNAL BLESSINGS IN YOUR LIFE NOW AND ALWAYS.

IF YOU SAY SO!

IF YOU SAY SO! I WILL PRAY ONLY TO OUR HEAVENLY FATHER WHOSE NAME ALONE IS HOLY.
Matthew 6:9

IF YOU SAY SO! I WILL LOVE OUR HEAVENLY FATHER WITH ALL MY HEART, WITH ALL MY SOUL, WITH ALL MY MIND AND WITH ALL MY STRENGTH.
Matthew 12:30

IF YOU SAY SO! I WILL LOVE MY NEIGHBOUR AS I LOVE MYSELF.
Matthew 12:31

IF YOU SAY SO! I WILL DO JUSTLY, I WILL LOVE MERCY, AND I WILL WALK HUMBLY BEFORE MY HEAVENLY FATHER.
Micah 6:8

IF YOU SAY SO! I WILL SEEK FIRST THE KINGDOM OF OUR HEAVENLY FATHER AND HIS RIGHTEOUSNESS, AND ALL I HAVE NEED OF WILL BE ADDED TO ME.
Matthew 6:33

IF YOU SAY SO! I WILL PUT MY TRUST IN OUR HEAVENLY FATHER AND NOT IN MY FELLOW MAN.
Psalm 118:8

IF YOU SAY SO! I WILL RESPECT AND PRAISE MY HEAVENLY FATHER AND KEEP HIS COMMANDS BECAUSE THIS IS MY RIGHTEOUS DUTY.
Ecclesiastes 12:13

IF YOU SAY SO PRECIOUS JESUS, I WILL TAKE YOU AT YOUR WORD. IF YOU SAY SO! I WILL SEEK YOU WITH ALL MY MIND WITH ALL MY HEART WITH ALL MY SOUL AND WITH ALL MY STRENGTH. I GIVE YOU ALL OF MY PRAISE AND ALL OF MY HONOUR NOW AND FOREVERMORE. AMEN AND AMEN.

WHAT CAN I DO TO LET YOU KNOW THAT I LOVE YOU?

WHAT CAN I DO TO LET YOU KNOW THAT I LOVE YOU? DO I HAVE TO SHOUT IT OUT LOUD LIKE A STORM BURSTING THROUGH THE CLOUD?

WHAT CAN I DO TO LET YOU KNOW THAT I LOVE YOU? DO I HAVE TO HOLD YOU CLOSE AND WHISPER IN YOUR EAR HOW MUCH I REALLY DO CARE?

WHAT CAN I DO TO LET YOU KNOW THAT I LOVE YOU? DO I HAVE TO HOLD YOUR HAND AND WRITE ON YOUR PALM OUR FUTURE PLAN?

WHAT CAN I DO TO LET YOU KNOW THAT I LOVE YOU? DO I HAVE TO KISS YOUR LIPS AS I GENTLY TOUCH YOUR FINGER TIPS?

WHAT CAN I DO TO LET YOU KNOW THAT I LOVE YOU? DO I HAVE TO GREET YOU WITH A SMILE AS WE TRAVEL MILE AFTER MILE?

WHAT CAN I DO TO LET YOU KNOW THAT I LOVE YOU? DO I HAVE TO HOLD YOU TIGHT AND GENTLY SQUEEZE YOU WITH ALL MY MIGHT?

WHAT CAN I DO TO LET YOU KNOW THAT I LOVE YOU? DO I HAVE TO LOOK INTO YOUR EYES AND TELL YOU I LOVE YOU AS MY HEART CRIES?

PLEASE LET ME KNOW WHAT I HAVE TO DO TO LET YOU KNOW THAT I LOVE YOU. ONE THING IS FOR SURE IF YOU LOVE ME AS MUCH AS I LOVE YOU, OUR HEARTS WILL BE FOREVER SET FREE.

I LOVE IT WHEN

I LOVE IT WHEN YOU HOLD ME TIGHT, I CAN FEEL YOUR BODY SAYING EVERYTHING IS GOING TO BE ALRIGHT.

I LOVE IT WHEN YOU WHISPER IN MY EAR, I CAN FEEL YOUR BODY DRAWING ME EVER SO NEAR AND TELLING ME HOW MUCH YOU CARE.

I LOVE IT WHEN YOU HOLD MY HAND, I CAN FEEL YOUR LOVE AND I CAN TRULY UNDERSTAND WHAT IS IN OUR ETERNAL PLAN.

I LOVE IT WHEN YOU LOOK INTO MY EYES, I CAN SEE YOUR SOUL AND I CAN SEE THE FASCINATING STORIES UNTOLD.

I LOVE IT WHEN YOU KISS MY LIPS, I CAN FEEL THE PLEASURE ALL THE WAY TO MY FINGER TIPS.

I LOVE IT WHEN YOU SMILE, I CAN FEEL THE PLEASURE MILE AFTER MILE, AFTER MILE.

I LOVE IT WHEN YOU SAY YOU CARE AND I CAN FEEL YOU DRIVING OUT ALL OF MY FEAR.

SWEET LADY, I AM BLESSED TO HAVE YOU AS MY WIFE. THE ONLY THING I WOULD CHANGE, I WOULD HAVE MARRIED YOU A LITTLE SOONER. THANK YOU FOR CHOOSING ME AND THANK YOU FOR ALLOWING MY HEART TO LOVE FREELY AGAIN. GOD BLESS YOU NOW AND ALWAYS. SWEET LADY, I APPRECIATE YOU. AMEN AND AMEN.

I AM IN LOVE WITH YOU SWEET LADY

YOU MAY THINK THAT I DON'T CARE, BUT PLEASE DO NOT FEAR, BECAUSE I AM IN LOVE WITH YOU SWEET LADY.

I WISH YOU COULD SEE WITHIN MY HEART, THE WAY I TREASURE YOU MY SWEETHEART, I KNOW YOU WILL NEVER DEPART, BECAUSE I AM IN LOVE WITH YOU SWEET LADY.

I WISH YOU ONLY KNEW, THE GOOD THINGS I HAVE IN STORE FOR YOU, BECAUSE I AM IN LOVE WITH YOU SWEET LADY.

I HOPE YOU REALIZE YOUR UNIQUENESS, THEREIN LIES YOUR SWEETNESS, BECAUSE I AM IN LOVE WITH YOU SWEET LADY.

AS TIME GOES BY, I AM GLAD I KISSED YOU AND HERE IS WHY, BECAUSE I AM IN LOVE WITH YOU SWEET LADY.

ONE THING IS FOR SURE, I FOUND A SWEET LADY I COULD TREASURE WHEN YOU OPENED MY HEART'S DOOR, BECAUSE I AM IN LOVE WITH YOU SWEET LADY.

I LOVE YOUR SWEET SMILE AND I WILL TREASURE IT ALONG WITH YOUR SWEET SIMPLE STYLE, BECAUSE I AM IN LOVE WITH YOU SWEET LADY.

FOR ALWAYS.

I AM GOING TO LOVE YOU FOREVER

I AM GOING TO LOVE YOU FOREVER WOULD YOU PROMISE TO STAY? I AM GOING TO LOVE YOU FOREVER WOULD YOU PROMISE TO NEVER SWAY?

I AM GOING TO LOVE YOU FOREVER WOULD YOU PROMISE TO BE MINE? I AM GOING TO LOVE YOU FOREVER WOULD YOU PROMISE TO BE THERE FOR ALL TIME?

I AM GOING TO LOVE YOU FOREVER WOULD YOU PROMISE TO BE TRUE? I AM GOING TO LOVE YOU FOREVER WOULD YOU PROMISE MY TEARS WOULD BE FEW?

I AM GOING TO LOVE YOU FOREVER WOULD YOU PROMISE TO BE KIND? I AM GOING TO LOVE YOU FOREVER WOULD YOU PROMISE YOU WILL ALWAYS BE MINE?

I AM GOING TO LOVE YOU FOREVER WOULD YOU PROMISE TO ALWAYS BE MY FRIEND? I AM GOING TO LOVE YOU FOREVER WOULD YOU PROMISE OUR LOVE WILL NEVER END?

I AM GOING TO LOVE YOU FOREVER WOULD YOU PROMISE TO HOLD ME CLOSE? I AM GOING TO LOVE YOU FOREVER WOULD YOU PROMISE TO LOVE ME THE MOST (EXCEPT FOR JESUS)?

I AM GOING TO LOVE YOU FOREVER THAT IS MY PROMISE TO YOU. I AM GOING TO LOVE YOU FOREVER THAT IS THE PROMISE I HAVE MADE TO YOU.

THERE IS NOTHING MORE PRECIOUS THAN LOVING SOMEONE. THE QUESTION IS, IS THAT SOMEONE GOING TO LOVE YOU BACK IN THE SAME WAY? ALL I KNOW IS TRUE LOVE NEVER DIES. TRUE LOVE WOULD DIE FOR YOU, JUST ASK PRECIOUS JESUS.

PLEASE BLESS HER PRECIOUS LORD JESUS I PRAY

PLEASE BLESS HER PRECIOUS LORD JESUS I PRAY. PLEASE BLESS HER EVERY SECOND OF EVERY DAY I PRAY. PLEASE BLESS HER FOREVER I PRAY.

PLEASE BLESS HER PRECIOUS LORD JESUS I PRAY. PLEASE BLESS HER EVERY MINUTE OF EVERY DAY I PRAY. PLEASE BLESS HER FOREVER I PRAY.

PLEASE BLESS HER PRECIOUS LORD JESUS I PRAY. PLEASE BLESS HER EVERY HOUR OF EVERY DAY I PRAY. PLEASE BLESS HER FOREVER I PRAY.

PLEASE BLESS HER PRECIOUS LORD JESUS I PRAY. PLEASE BLESS HER EVERY MONTH I PRAY. PLEASE BLESS HER FOREVER I PRAY.

PLEASE BLESS HER PRECIOUS LORD JESUS I PRAY. PLEASE BLESS HER EVERY YEAR I PRAY. PLEASE BLESS HER FOREVER I PRAY.

PLEASE BLESS HER PRECIOUS LORD JESUS I PRAY. PLEASE BLESS HER EVERY DECADE I PRAY. PLEASE BLESS HER FOREVER I PRAY.

PLEASE BLESS HER PRECIOUS LORD JESUS I PRAY. PLEASE BLESS HER EVERY CENTURY I PRAY. PLEASE BLESS HER FOREVER I PRAY.

PRECIOUS LORD JESUS, WE ALL DESPERATELY NEED YOUR BLESSINGS. SHE NEEDS YOUR BLESSINGS IN EVERY ASPECT OF HER LIFE. RIGHT NOW, PRECIOUS LORD JESUS, SHE NEEDS YOUR BLESSINGS SPIRITUALLY, EMOTIONALLY, PHYSICALLY AND FINANCIALLY. WE BELIEVE IN YOU PRECIOUS LORD JESUS AND WE BELIEVE ALL YOUR PROMISES TO BE FAITHFUL AND TRUE. WE GIVE YOU ALL OF OUR PRAISE AND ALL OF THE GLORY, NOW AND ALWAYS. AMEN AND AMEN.

JEREMIAH 29:11 (NIV) *For I know the plans I have for you, declares the Lord, plans to prosper you and not to harm you, plans to give you hope and a future.*

MAKE JESUS YOUR FIRST LOVE

MAKE JESUS YOUR FIRST LOVE BECAUSE HE IS THE ONE THAT PROTECTS YOU FROM ABOVE.

MAKE JESUS YOUR FIRST LOVE BECAUSE HE LAVISHES YOU WITH HIS ETERNAL LOVE.

MAKE JESUS YOUR FIRST LOVE BECAUSE HE WILL REST ON YOU LIKE A GENTLE DOVE.

MAKE JESUS YOUR FIRST LOVE BECAUSE HE IS ALWAYS READY TO GIVE SO YOU AND I CAN LIVE.

MAKE JESUS YOUR FIRST LOVE BECAUSE HE IS WILLING TO TAKE THE BLAME FOR OUR AWFUL SHAME.

MAKE JESUS YOUR FIRST LOVE BECAUSE HE IS THE ONLY ONE WHO TRULY UNDERSTANDS.

MAKE JESUS YOUR FIRST LOVE BECAUSE IN HIM YOU WILL FIND ETERNAL DESTINY SUBLIME.

THANK YOU FOR LOVING US PRECIOUS LORD JESUS. WE CANNOT REPAY THE AWESOME LOVE YOU HAVE BESTOWED ON US. THEREFORE, WE WILL GIVE YOU ALL OF OUR PRAISE AND ALL THE GLORY, NOW AND FOREVERMORE. AMEN AND AMEN.

I LONG

I LONG TO LOOK INTO YOUR EYES AND I LONG TO GIVE YOU AN ETERNAL PRIZE.

I LONG TO TOUCH YOU TENDERLY AND I LONG TO HOLD YOU SO CLOSE TO ME.

I LONG TO WHISPER IN YOUR EAR AND I LONG TO TELL YOU HOW MUCH I REALLY CARE.

I LONG TO HOLD YOUR HAND AND I LONG TO TELL YOU OUR FUTURE PLAN.

I LONG TO WALK BESIDE YOU AND I LONG TO TALK TO YOU TOO.

I LONG TO KISS YOUR TENDER LIPS AND I LONG TO PLACE MY HANDS TENDERLY ON YOUR HIPS.

I LONG TO TELL YOU HOW MUCH I LOVE YOU AND I LONG TO SHOW YOU HOW MUCH I REALLY DO.

SWEET LADY, IF I DID NOT MEET YOU, I WOULD NOT HAVE KNOWN WHAT I WAS HOLDING INSIDE. THANK YOU FOR BEING PATIENT WITH ME. BE BLESSED IN THE MOST PRECIOUS NAME OF JESUS. AMEN AND AMEN.

PLEASE GIVE ME A LITTLE TIME

PLEASE GIVE ME A LITTLE TIME AND I PROMISE I WILL MAKE YOU MINE.

PLEASE GIVE ME A LITTLE TIME AND I PROMISE WE WILL SIP SOME RED OR WHITE WINE.

PLEASE GIVE ME A LITTLE TIME AND I PROMISE FOREVER WE WILL DINE.

PLEASE GIVE ME A LITTLE TIME AND I PROMISE BY THE GRACE OF GOD EVERYTHING WILL BE FINE.

PLEASE GIVE ME A LITTLE TIME AND I PROMISE NO SWEETER LOVE YOU WILL FIND.

PLEASE GIVE ME A LITTLE TIME AND I PROMISE THAT OUR LOVE WILL FOREVER BE ENTWINED.

PLEASE GIVE ME A LITTLE TIME AND I PROMISE YOU WILL FOREVER BE ON MY MIND.

I AM ASKING OF YOU SWEET LADY TO GIVE ME A LITTLE TIME AND I PROMISE YOU THAT YOU WILL ALWAYS BE MINE. GOD BLESS AND KEEP YOU ALWAYS. AMEN AND AMEN.

HAPPY NEW YEAR

HAPPY NEW YEAR WITH ALL MY LOVE. I PRAY PRECIOUS JESUS WILL BLESS YOU FROM HIS THRONE UP ABOVE.

HAPPY NEW YEAR FROM THE DEPTH OF MY HEART. I PROMISE YOU, FROM MY HEART YOU WILL NEVER DEPART.

HAPPY NEW YEAR WITH BOUNTIFUL BLESSINGS. PLEASE LET PRECIOUS JESUS TEACH YOU HIS ETERNAL LESSONS.

HAPPY NEW YEAR WITH JOY AND HOPE. REACH OUT TO PRECIOUS JESUS AND HE WILL BROADEN YOUR SCOPE.

HAPPY NEW YEAR WITH GOODNESS AND GRACE. PLEASE KEEP YOUR FOCUS ON PRECIOUS JESUS GLORIOUS FACE.

HAPPY NEW YEAR WITH MERCY AND TRUTH. CALL UPON PRECIOUS JESUS AND HE WILL RENEW YOUR YOUTH.

HAPPY NEW YEAR WITH ALL MY LOVE. I PRAY THE HOLY SPIRIT WILL REST UPON YOU LIKE A GENTLE DOVE.

HAPPY NEW YEAR. I AM PRAYING FOR YOU TO HAVE THE BEST YEAR EVER. I HOPE AND PRAY ALL OF GOD'S RICH AND WONDERFUL BLESSINGS IN YOUR LIFE. I LOVE YOU ALWAYS AND FOREVER. GOD BLESS YOU ALWAYS.

TRUE LOVE

TRUE LOVE IS PATIENT AND KIND. TRUE LOVE IS NEVER BLIND.

TRUE LOVE IS GIVING AND SHARING. TRUE LOVE IS ALWAYS CARING.

TRUE LOVE IS GENTLE AND UNDERSTANDING. TRUE LOVE IS NEVER DEMANDING.

TRUE LOVE IS BRIGHT AND CLEAN. TRUE LOVE IS NEVER MEAN.

TRUE LOVE IS RICH AND SWEET. TRUE LOVE IS EVER SO NEAT.

TRUE LOVE IS MEEK AND MILD. TRUE LOVE IS GREETING YOU WITH A SMILE.

TRUE LOVE IS HONOURABLE AND RESPECTABLE. TRUE LOVE IS NEVER DESPICABLE.

TRUE LOVE IS SO VAST AND EVER SO WIDE. TRUE LOVE IS LIKE THE OCEAN'S TIDE. TRUE LOVE YOU OR I CAN NEVER HIDE. I HAVE FOUND IN YOU A TRUE LOVE AND I AM GOING TO CHERISH YOU BECAUSE YOU WERE SENT TO ME FROM MY MASTER UP ABOVE. YOU ARE MY TRUE LOVE.

LIKE I CAN'T

PLEASE LOVE HER ETERNALLY LIKE I CAN'T, PRECIOUS LORD JESUS I PRAY.

PLEASE PROTECT HER ETERNALLY LIKE I CAN'T, PRECIOUS LORD JESUS I PRAY.

PLEASE HOLD HER ETERNALLY LIKE I CAN'T, PRECIOUS LORD JESUS I PRAY.

PLEASE COMFORT HER ETERNALLY LIKE I CAN'T, PRECIOUS LORD JESUS I PRAY.

PLEASE CARESS HER ETERNALLY LIKE I CAN'T, PRECIOUS LORD JESUS I PRAY.

PLEASE CHERISH HER ETERNALLY LIKE I CAN'T, PRECIOUS LORD JESUS I PRAY.

PLEASE BLESS HER ETERNALLY LIKE I CAN'T, PRECIOUS LORD JESUS I PRAY.

WELL YOUNG LADY, THESE ARE ALL THE THINGS I WOULD WANT TO DO FOR YOU, BUT I CAN'T. I CAN FULFILL THEM ONLY PARTIALLY,

BUT OUR PRECIOUS LORD JESUS CAN FULFILL THEM ETERNALLY. I
HOPE AND PRAY ALL OF GOD'S RICH AND WONDERFUL BLESSINGS
IN YOUR LIFE, NOW AND ALWAYS. I CAN'T TURN MY LOVE OFF.
LOVE ALWAYS.

WHEN I SAY I DO

IF I SHOULD EVER KISS YOU FOR ANY LENGTH OF TIME, IT IS WHEN I SAY I DO.

IF I SHOULD EVER HOLD YOUR HAND FOR ANY LENGTH OF TIME, IT IS WHEN I SAY I DO.

IF I SHOULD EVER WALK WITH YOU FOR ANY LENGTH OF TIME, IT IS WHEN I SAY I DO.

IF I SHOULD EVER TALK WITH YOU FOR ANY LENGTH OF TIME, IT IS WHEN I SAY I DO.

IF I SHOULD EVER CHERISH YOU FOR ANY LENGTH OF TIME, IT IS WHEN I SAY I DO.

IF I SHOULD EVER SMILE WITH YOU FOR ANY LENGTH OF TIME, IT IS WHEN I SAY I DO.

IF I SHOULD EVER TELL YOU, I LOVE YOU FOR ANY LENGTH OF TIME, IT IS WHEN I SAY I DO.

SWEET LADY, ALL I CAN SAY IS, IF WE ARE TRULY IN LOVE THEN IN TIME, I WILL SAY I DO. AS THE SAYING GOES, HURRY MAKES WORRY. HUSH SWEET LADY, WE DON'T HAVE TO WORRY. GOD BLESS YOU ALWAYS AND FOREVER.

PLEASE KEEP YOUR HEART FOR ME

PLEASE KEEP YOUR HEART FOR ME. I WILL COME FOR IT. PLEASE KEEP YOUR HEART FOR ME. I PROMISE YOU WILL NEVER REGRET IT.

PLEASE KEEP YOUR HEART FOR ME. I WILL ALWAYS CHERISH IT. PLEASE KEEP YOUR HEART FOR ME. I WILL ALWAYS REPLENISH IT.

PLEASE KEEP YOUR HEART FOR ME. I WILL ALWAYS GUARD IT. PLEASE KEEP YOUR HEART FOR ME. I WILL ALWAYS HAVE THE UTMOST REGARDS FOR IT.

PLEASE KEEP YOUR HEART FOR ME. I WILL ALWAYS BE WARM TO IT. PLEASE KEEP YOUR HEART FOR ME. I WILL NEVER BRING ANY HARM TO IT.

PLEASE KEEP YOUR HEART FOR ME. I WILL ALWAYS BE KIND TO IT. PLEASE KEEP YOUR HEART FOR ME. I WILL ALWAYS HAVE TIME FOR IT.

PLEASE KEEP YOUR HEART FOR ME. I WILL ALWAYS HOLD IT. PLEASE KEEP YOUR HEART FOR ME. I PROMISE I WILL NEVER LET GO OF IT.

PLEASE KEEP YOUR HEART FOR ME. I WILL ALWAYS LOVE IT. PLEASE KEEP YOUR HEART FOR ME. I PROMISE I WILL ONLY PUT PRECIOUS JESUS ABOVE IT.

IF YOU GIVE ME YOUR HEART, I PROMISE YOU SWEET LADY, I WILL ALWAYS CHERISH IT, I WILL ALWAYS REPLENISH IT AND I WILL ALWAYS PROTECT IT. GOD BLESS YOU NOW AND ALWAYS. LOVE ALWAYS.

WHEN

WHEN YOU CALL, I WILL ANSWER YOU SWEET LADY.

WHEN YOU SPEAK, I WILL LISTEN TO YOU SWEET LADY.

WHEN YOU ARE COLD, I WILL KEEP YOU WARM IN MY ARMS SWEET LADY.

WHEN YOU HURT, I WILL COMFORT YOU SWEET LADY.

WHEN YOU CRY, I WILL KISS YOUR TEARS AWAY SWEET LADY.

WHEN YOU SMILE, I WILL SMILE WITH YOU SWEET LADY.

WHEN YOU LOVE, I WILL ALWAYS LOVE YOU SWEET LADY.

THERE IS NOTHING SWEETER THAN LOVE. LOVE WILL MAKE THE WEAK STRONG, THE POOR RICH AND THE IGNORANT WISE. TRUE LOVE IS ALL WE NEED. WE HAVE THAT TRUE LOVE BECAUSE OF PRECIOUS JESUS. AMEN AND AMEN.

IN YOU

THERE IS A SWEETNESS IN YOU, I HOPE AND PRAY YOU WILL NEVER LOSE. THERE IS A KINDNESS IN YOU AND IT'S BECAUSE OF THE MASTER YOU CHOOSE.

THERE IS A GENTLENESS IN YOU, I HOPE AND PRAY YOU WILL NEVER LOSE. THERE IS A MEEKNESS IN YOU AND IT'S BECAUSE OF THE MASTER YOU CHOOSE.

THERE IS A HAPPINESS IN YOU, I HOPE AND PRAY YOU WILL NEVER LOSE. THERE IS A JOYFULNESS IN YOU AND IT'S BECAUSE OF THE MASTER YOU CHOOSE.

THERE IS A HUMBLENESS IN YOU, I HOPE AND PRAY YOU WILL NEVER LOSE. THERE IS A COMELINESS IN YOU AND IT'S BECAUSE OF THE MASTER YOU CHOOSE.

THERE IS A GOODNESS IN YOU, I HOPE AND PRAY YOU WILL NEVER LOSE. THERE IS A PERSUASIVENESS IN YOU AND IT'S BECAUSE OF THE MASTER YOU CHOOSE.

THERE IS A WORTHINESS IN YOU, I HOPE AND PRAY YOU WILL NEVER LOSE. THERE IS A TRUTHFULNESS IN YOU AND IT'S BECAUSE OF THE MASTER YOU CHOOSE.

THERE IS A LOVE IN YOU, I HOPE AND PRAY YOU WILL NEVER LOSE. THERE IS A LOVINGKINDNESS IN YOU AND IT'S BECAUSE OF THE MASTER YOU CHOOSE.

SWEET LADY I HAVE BEEN THINKING ABOUT YOU ALL DAY, WHAT ELSE IS NEW. I HAVE COME TO THE REALIZATION THAT IT IS UNFAIR OF ME TO EXPECT YOU TO LOVE ME IN THE SAME WAY IN WHICH I LOVE YOU. I WANT YOU TO KNOW THAT THIS IS BY NO MEANS A GOOD BYE LETTER OR ANYTHING OF THE SORT.

SWEET LADY IF FRIENDSHIP IS ALL YOU CAN OFFER, I WILL SETTLE FOR IT. LET IT BE KNOWN, I WILL ALWAYS BE THERE FOR YOU. I DO LOVE YOU AND I CAN'T TURN IT OFF. BUT I DO KNOW IF YOU TRULY LOVE SOMEONE, LIKE I LOVE YOU, I HAVE TO SET YOU FREE. THERE IS NO LOSS IN EMBRACING A FRIENDSHIP FOR ALL ETERNITY.

I HOPE AND PRAY OUR HEAVENLY FATHER'S RICH AND ETERNAL BLESSINGS IN ALL THAT YOU DO. LOVE ALWAYS SWEET LADY.

YOUR LOVE SWEET LADY

I WANT YOUR LOVE WITH EVERY STEP THAT I TAKE. I WANT YOUR LOVE WITH EVERY DECISION THAT I MAKE. SWEET LADY I WANT YOUR LOVE.

I DESIRE YOUR LOVE WITH EVERY STEP THAT I TAKE. I DESIRE YOUR LOVE WITH EVERY DECISION THAT I MAKE. SWEET LADY I DESIRE YOUR LOVE.

I NEED YOUR LOVE WITH EVERY STEP THAT I TAKE. I NEED YOUR LOVE WITH EVERY DECISION THAT I MAKE. SWEET LADY I NEED YOUR LOVE.

I CHERISH YOUR LOVE WITH EVERY STEP THAT I TAKE. I CHERISH YOUR LOVE WITH EVERY DECISION THAT I MAKE. SWEET LADY I CHERISH YOUR LOVE.

I CRAVE YOUR LOVE WITH EVERY STEP THAT I TAKE. I CRAVE YOUR LOVE WITH EVERY DECISION THAT I MAKE. SWEET LADY I CRAVE YOUR LOVE.

I FEEL YOUR LOVE WITH EVERY STEP THAT I TAKE. I FEEL YOUR LOVE WITH EVERY DECISION THAT I MAKE. SWEET LADY I FEEL YOUR LOVE.

I TASTE YOUR LOVE WITH EVERY STEP THAT I TAKE. I TASTE YOUR LOVE WITH EVERY DECISION THAT I MAKE. SWEET LADY I TASTE YOUR LOVE.

SWEET LADY WITH EVERY STEP THAT I TAKE AND WITH EVERY DECISION THAT I MAKE, I AM GOING TO NEED YOUR LOVE. I HOPE AND PRAY YOU WILL NEED MY LOVE TOO. BUT THE LOVE OF PRECIOUS JESUS COMES FIRST. LOVE ALWAYS.

THE BEST REVENGE IS
NO REVENGE AT ALL

THE BEST REVENGE IS NO REVENGE AT ALL. DON'T GIVE YOUR ENEMY ANY AMMUNITION TO CONTRIBUTE TO YOUR DEMOLITION.

THE BEST REVENGE IS NO REVENGE AT ALL. DON'T PROVIDE YOUR ENEMY WITH FIRE TO MAKE YOUR LIFE DIRE.

THE BEST REVENGE IS NO REVENGE AT ALL. DON'T REFUSE TO TURN THE OTHER CHEEK, IT CAN BE ACCOMPLISHED ONLY BY THE HUMBLE AND THE MEEK.

THE BEST REVENGE IS NO REVENGE AT ALL. DON'T REFUSE TO HELP YOUR ENEMY WHEN THEY FALL BECAUSE YOU WILL BE ANSWERING PRECIOUS JESUS RIGHTEOUS CALL.

THE BEST REVENGE IS NO REVENGE AT ALL. DON'T REFUSE TO GIVE YOUR ENEMY WATER TO DRINK, IN SO DOING YOU MAY FORM AN ETERNAL LINK.

THE BEST REVENGE IS NO REVENGE AT ALL. DON'T REFUSE TO GIVE YOUR ENEMY BREAD TO EAT, IN SO DOING YOU MAY FIND A SWEET RETREAT.

THE BEST REVENGE IS NO REVENGE AT ALL. DON'T REFUSE TO SHOW YOUR ENEMY LOVE BECAUSE THAT IS WHAT IS REQUIRED FROM HEAVEN ABOVE.

WORDS TO THE WISE CHILDREN OF OUR HEAVENLY FATHER, THE BEST REVENGE IS NO REVENGE AT ALL. OUR HEAVENLY FATHER IS THE ONLY ONE WHO CAN AVENGE US. TO GOD BE THE GLORY, NOW AND FOREVERMORE. AMEN AND AMEN.

I GIVE MY HEART TO YOU

I GIVE MY HEART TO YOU. I WILL GIVE IT TO YOU WILLINGLY WITHOUT A FIGHT AND I AM PRAYING EVERYTHING WILL BE ALRIGHT.

I GIVE MY HEART TO YOU. I WILL PLACE IT GENTLY IN YOUR CARE AND I AM PRAYING THAT YOU WILL ALWAYS BE NEAR.

I GIVE MY HEART TO YOU. I WILL GIVE IT TO YOU WITHOUT RESERVATION AND I AM PRAYING WE WILL BOTH HAVE THE SAME ETERNAL DESTINATION.

I GIVE MY HEART TO YOU. I WILL PLACE IT BY YOUR SIDE AND I AM PRAYING THERE IT WILL FOREVER ABIDE.

I GIVE MY HEART TO YOU. I WILL GIVE IT TO YOU SO YOU CAN REACH AND I AM PRAYING FOR THE GOOD SO EACH OTHER WE CAN TEACH.

I GIVE MY HEART TO YOU. I WILL PLACE IT BESIDE YOU WITH GOOD INTENTION AND I AM PRAYING I WILL WIN YOUR EVERLASTING ATTENTION.

I GIVE MY HEART TO YOU. I WILL GIVE IT TO YOU WITH ALL MY LOVE AND I AM PRAYING IT WILL REFLECT MY PRECIOUS LORD JESUS UP ABOVE.

I AM AWAKE AT 3:45AM JUST READING SCRIPTURE AND THINKING ABOUT YOU. I AM THANKFUL THAT I MET YOU. YOU HAVE GIVEN ME A MEANINGFUL PERSPECTIVE AND OUTLOOK IN THIS PERIOD OF MY LIFE. I AM SO THANKFUL FOR YOU. I PRAY OUR HEAVENLY FATHER'S RICH AND BOUNTIFUL BLESSINGS IN OUR LIVES, NOW AND ALWAYS. AMEN AND AMEN.

I AM ALWAYS HERE FOR YOU

I AM ALWAYS HERE FOR YOU AND I WILL ALWAYS BE NEAR TO YOU.

I AM ALWAYS BESIDE YOU READY AND WILLING TO GUIDE YOU.

I AM ALWAYS WALKING WITH YOU AND ALWAYS WANTING TO TALK TO YOU.

I AM ALWAYS CARING FOR YOU AND I AM ALWAYS SHARING WITH YOU.

I AM ALWAYS PROVIDING FOR YOU AND I AM ALWAYS GUIDING YOU.

I AM ALWAYS PRAYING FOR YOU AND I AM ALWAYS CHEERING FOR YOU.

I AM ALWAYS LOVING YOU AND I AM ALWAYS HOVERING OVER YOU.

I THANK YOU PRECIOUS HOLY FATHER FOR YOUR LOVING KINDNESS AND YOUR TENDER MERCIES TOWARDS ME. I GIVE YOU ALL OF MY PRAISE AND ALL THE GLORY, NOW AND ALWAYS. AMEN AND AMEN.

FOR YOU

I LONG FOR YOU. I HOPE YOU LONG FOR ME TOO.

MY HEART YEARNS FOR YOU. I HOPE YOUR HEART YEARNS FOR ME TOO.

MY ARMS ARE OPEN WIDE FOR YOU. I HOPE YOUR ARMS ARE OPEN WIDE FOR ME TOO.

MY EYES ARE ALWAYS SEARCHING FOR YOU. I HOPE YOUR EYES SEARCH FOR ME TOO.

MY MIND ASKS FOR YOU. I HOPE YOUR MIND ASKS FOR ME TOO.

MY LIPS LONG FOR YOUR KISS. I HOPE YOUR LIPS LONG FOR MY KISS TOO.

MY DESIRE IS FOR YOU. I HOPE YOUR DESIRE IS FOR ME TOO.

QUARTER TO FIVE IN THE MORNING AND YOU ARE ON MY MIND AND IN MY THOUGHTS. I HOPE I AM IN YOUR THOUGHTS AND ON YOUR MIND TOO. GOD BLESS YOU ALWAYS.

I WANT YOU BESIDE ME
PRECIOUS JESUS

I WANT YOU BESIDE ME PRECIOUS JESUS WHEREVER I GO. I WANT YOU BESIDE ME PRECIOUS JESUS AS YOU HELP ME TO GROW.

I WANT YOU BESIDE ME PRECIOUS JESUS EARLY IN THE MORNING. I WANT YOU BESIDE ME PRECIOUS JESUS AT THE DAY'S GLORIOUS ADORNING.

I WANT YOU BESIDE ME PRECIOUS JESUS IN THE MIDDLE OF DAY. I WANT YOU BESIDE ME PRECIOUS JESUS AS WE WALK ALONG THE WAY.

I WANT YOU BESIDE ME PRECIOUS JESUS IN THE EVENING HOURS. I WANT YOU BESIDE ME PRECIOUS JESUS WHEN THE HEAVEN'S POUR DOWN ITS SHOWERS.

I WANT YOU BESIDE ME PRECIOUS JESUS IN THE MIDDLE OF THE NIGHT. I WANT YOU BESIDE ME PRECIOUS JESUS SO I CAN ALWAYS HOLD ONTO YOU SO TIGHT.

I WANT YOU BESIDE ME PRECIOUS JESUS EVERY HOUR OF EVERY DAY. I WANT YOU BESIDE ME PRECIOUS JESUS THIS IS WHAT I PRAY.

I WANT YOU BESIDE ME PRECIOUS JESUS FOR ALL TIME. I WANT YOU BESIDE ME PRECIOUS JESUS BECAUSE YOU PROMISED YOU WILL ALWAYS BE MINE.

I THANK YOU PRECIOUS LORD FOR ALWAYS BEING BESIDE ME. I THANK YOU FOR YOUR ENCOURAGEMENT AND FOR ALL YOUR BOUNTIFUL BENEFITS TOWARDS ME. I WILLINGLY GIVE YOU ALL OF MY PRAISE NOW AND ALWAYS. AMEN AND AMEN.

MY LOVE FOR YOU

MY LOVE FOR YOU WILL NEVER END BECAUSE YOU SWEET LADY ARE MY BEST FRIEND.

MY LOVE FOR YOU WILL NEVER DIE BECAUSE BESIDE YOU SWEET LADY I WILL ALWAYS LIE.

MY LOVE FOR YOU WILL NEVER SWAY BECAUSE YOU SWEET LADY WILL LEAD ME IN THE RIGHT WAY.

MY LOVE FOR YOU WILL NEVER CHANGE BECAUSE YOU SWEET LADY WILL NEVER BE STRANGE.

MY LOVE FOR YOU WILL NEVER HURT BECAUSE YOU SWEET LADY ARE THE SWEETEST LADY ON THE WHOLE EARTH.

MY LOVE FOR YOU WILL NEVER FEAR BECAUSE FOR YOU SWEET LADY I WILL ALWAYS CARE.

MY LOVE FOR YOU WILL ALWAYS LIVE BECAUSE TO YOU SWEET LADY MY LOVE I WILL ALWAYS GIVE.

YOU HAVE MY LOVE ALWAYS, IF YOU WANT. GOD BLESS YOU ALWAYS.

I CHOOSE YOU

I CHOOSE YOU TO COME TO AND I WON'T EVER RUN AWAY FROM YOU. I CHOOSE YOU.

I CHOOSE YOU TO TALK TO AND I WON'T EVER REMAIN SILENT TOWARDS YOU. I CHOOSE YOU.

I CHOOSE YOU TO WALK WITH AND I WON'T EVER WALK AWAY FROM YOU. I CHOOSE YOU.

I CHOOSE YOU TO SMILE WITH AND I WON'T EVER FROWN UPON YOU. I CHOOSE YOU.

I CHOOSE YOU TO HOLD CLOSE AND I REFUSE TO LET GO OF YOU. I CHOOSE YOU.

I CHOOSE YOU TO CHERISH AND I PRAY YOU WILL CHERISH ME TOO. I CHOOSE YOU.

I CHOOSE YOU TO LOVE AND I HOPE YOU CHOOSE TO LOVE ME TOO. I CHOOSE YOU.

WE ALL HAVE CHOICES TO MAKE. I CHOOSE YOU. I AM HOPING AND PRAYING THAT YOU WILL CHOOSE ME TOO. GOD BLESS YOU ALWAYS.

NOT FOR LACK OF LOVE

IT ISN'T FOR A LACK OF LOVE THAT WE ARE TORN APART, IT IS THE DIRECTION OF OUR HEART.

WE HAVE SHOWN GREAT RESPECT FOR EACH OTHER BUT THE DIRECTION OF OUR HEART HAS BECOME A BOTHER.

WE KNOW OUR LOVE FOR EACH OTHER WILL NEVER DIE BUT FOR EACH OTHER OUR HEARTS WILL ALWAYS CRY.

WE KNOW THAT THERE ARE DECISIONS TO BE MADE AND WITH THAT SAID, THERE IS A GREAT PRICE TO BE PAID.

WE KNOW THAT THERE IS ALWAYS HOPE, BUT HOW LONG CAN OUR HURTING HEART COPE.

WE KNOW THE JOY THAT LOVE CAN BRING AND I HOPE IT WILL NOT BE TOO LATE FOR A NEW SONG THAT WE BOTH CAN SING.

WE HAVE TO CHOOSE WHICH ROAD WE MUST TAKE AND I HOPE OUR HEARTS WON'T HAVE TO WORRY AND WON'T HAVE TO ACHE.

WELL YOUNG LADY WE HAVE SOME DECISIONS TO BE MADE. I HOPE WHEN IT IS ALL SAID AND DONE, WE ARE ON THE SAME PAGE. I THANK YOU FOR ALL THAT YOU HAVE DONE FOR ME AND I AM FOREVER GRATEFUL TO YOU FOR ALL THAT YOU DO. GOD BLESS YOU NOW AND ALWAYS IN THE PRECIOUS NAME OF JESUS. AMEN AND AMEN.

ALL OF ME

ALL OF ME IS LONGING FOR ALL OF YOU PRECIOUS LORD JESUS. ALL OF ME IS REACHING OUT TO ALL OF YOU PRECIOUS LORD JESUS.

ALL OF ME IS YEARNING FOR ALL OF YOU PRECIOUS LORD JESUS. ALL OF ME HAS A BURNING DESIRE FOR ALL OF YOU PRECIOUS LORD JESUS.

ALL OF ME WANTS TO BE CLOSE TO ALL OF YOU PRECIOUS LORD JESUS. ALL OF ME IS LONGING TO GO FROM COAST TO COAST WITH ALL OF YOU PRECIOUS LORD JESUS.

ALL OF ME WANTS TO DO MY BEST FOR ALL OF YOU PRECIOUS LORD JESUS. ALL OF ME CAN'T REST WITHOUT ALL OF YOU PRECIOUS LORD JESUS.

ALL OF ME IS ALWAYS SEARCHING FOR ALL OF YOU PRECIOUS LORD JESUS. ALL OF ME IS ALWAYS REACHING FOR ALL OF YOU PRECIOUS LORD JESUS.

ALL OF ME FEELS EMPTY WITHOUT ALL OF YOU PRECIOUS LORD JESUS. ALL OF ME CAN ACCOMPLISH PLENTY WITH ALL OF YOU PRECIOUS LORD JESUS.

ALL OF ME WILL GIVE MY ALL TO ALL OF YOU PRECIOUS LORD JESUS. ALL OF ME WILL ALWAYS BE A PART OF ALL OF YOU PRECIOUS LORD JESUS.

OFTEN TIMES PEOPLE FALL IN LOVE AND EVERYTHING SEEMS TO BE GOING SO WONDERFULLY. THEN SUDDENLY THINGS FALL APART AND MANY ARE LEFT WITH A BROKEN HEART. THEN COMES THE HURT AND THE PAIN AND NO ONE SEEMS TO GAIN. I CAN SAY FOR CERTAIN, IF YOU TRULY LOVE SOMEONE THERE WILL ALWAYS BE LOVE IN YOUR HEART FOR THAT PERSON. LOVE IS THE BEST THING GOD HAS EVER CREATED. GOD BLESS YOU ALWAYS.

IS THAT SOMEONE YOU?

I NEED SOMEONE TO WALK WITH ME ALONG THE WAY. I NEED SOMEONE TO BE WITH ME DAY BY DAY. IS THAT SOMEONE YOU?

I NEED SOME TO TALK WITH ME ALONG THE WAY. I NEED SOMEONE TO TALK TO ME EACH AND EVERY DAY. IS THAT SOMEONE YOU?

I NEED SOMEONE TO HOLD MY HAND ALONG THE WAY. I NEED SOMEONE TO HOLD MY HAND EACH AND EVERY DAY. IS THAT SOMEONE YOU?

I NEED SOMEONE TO GIVE ME HOPE ALONG THE WAY. I NEED SOMEONE TO HOPE WITH ME EACH AND EVERY DAY. IS THAT SOMEONE YOU?

I NEED SOMEONE TO TRUST ALONG THE WAY. I NEED SOMEONE I CAN TRUST EACH AND EVERY DAY. IS THAT SOMEONE YOU?

I NEED THAT SPECIAL SOMEONE TO LOVE ALONG THE WAY. I NEED THAT SPECIAL SOMEONE TO LOVE EACH AND EVERY DAY. IS THAT SPECIAL SOMEONE YOU?

I AM ALWAYS THINKING ABOUT YOU YOUNG LADY. WE HAVE CROSSED PATHS FOR A REASON. PLEASE STAY SAFE IN THE PRECIOUS ARMS OF JESUS. GOD BLESS YOU ALWAYS. AMEN AND AMEN.

YOU SAY YOU ARE OK BUT THAT IS NOT QUITE TRUE

WHEN I ASK IF YOU ARE OK, YOU SAY "I AM FINE", BUT I KNOW THAT IS NOT QUITE TRUE BECAUSE I CAN SEE THE MASTERS JOY IS NOT WITHIN YOU. YOU SAY YOU ARE OK BUT THAT IS NOT QUITE TRUE.

WHENEVER I SEE YOU SMILE, I DON'T SEE THE JOY TARRYING MILE AFTER MILE. YOU SAY YOU ARE OK BUT THAT IS NOT QUITE TRUE.

WHENEVER I HEAR YOU TALK TO ME IT IS NOT IN SYNC WITH THE WAY YOU WALK WITH ME. YOU SAY YOU ARE OK BUT THAT IS NOT QUITE TRUE.

WHENEVER I LOOK INTO YOUR EYES, YOU AVOID A PROLONGED GAZE AND EVERYTHING BECOMES A HAZE. YOU SAY YOU ARE OK BUT THAT IS NOT QUITE TRUE.

WHENEVER I TRY TO LISTEN TO YOUR HEART, I DON'T ALWAYS GET THE SOUND RIGHT FROM THE VERY START. YOU SAY YOU ARE OK BUT THAT IS NOT QUITE TRUE.

WHENEVER I AM HUGGING YOU, I FEEL LIKE I AM FALLING IN LOVE WITH YOU, WHY ARE YOU HIDING A LOVE SO TRUE. YOU SAY YOU ARE OK BUT THAT IS NOT QUITE TRUE.

WHENEVER I THINK OF YOU, I OFTEN SEE ONLY SHADOWS OF BLUE BUT ONE DAY I HOPE FOR YOU THAT ALL THINGS WILL BECOME NEW. YOU SAY YOU ARE OK BUT THAT IS NOT QUITE TRUE.

I HEAR YOU SAY YOU ARE OK ALL THE TIME, BUT DEEP WITHIN MY HEART I KNOW THAT IS NOT QUITE TRUE. PLEASE FORGIVE ME WHERE I HAVE FAILED YOU. I KNOW THERE IS A BRIGHT FUTURE AHEAD OF YOU. ALL YOU HAVE TO DO, IS SEEK YOUR MASTER'S PLAN AND HE WILL GUIDE YOU WITH HIS HOLY HAND. GOD BLESS YOU NOW AND ALWAYS. AMEN AND AMEN.

THIS IS WHY I LOVE YOU

YOU ARE KIND AND DEFINITELY ONE OF A KIND. THIS IS WHY I LOVE YOU.

YOU HAVE INNER BEAUTY AND YOU ARE READY TO LIVE OUT YOUR DUTY. THIS IS WHY I LOVE YOU.

YOU HAVE A LOVING HEART, EVER SO SWEET AND NEVER TART. THIS IS WHY I LOVE YOU.

YOU HAVE A SWEET SPIRIT, I BELIEVE, YOU HAVE PRECIOUS JESUS WITHIN IT. THIS IS WHY I LOVE YOU.

YOU HAVE A HOPE BEYOND TODAY, I SEE YOU STRIVE FOR IT DAY AFTER DAY. THIS IS WHY I LOVE YOU.

YOU NEVER COMPLAIN AS YOU WITHSTAND LIFE'S STINGING PAIN. THIS IS WHY I LOVE YOU.

YOU HAVE A LOVE SO TRUE, THAT IS WHAT'S SO UNIQUE ABOUT YOU. THIS IS WHY I LOVE YOU.

LIKE I SAY, IT IS SO EASY TO WRITE ABOUT YOU. YOU ARE UNIQUE AND SO SPECIAL AND SO SWEET. PLEASE DON'T LET THIS WORLD TARNISH YOU. JUST BE TRUE. LOVE ALWAYS. GOD BLESS YOU ALWAYS.

ABOUT THE AUTHOR

My name is Halcourth Delando O'Gilvie, I was born on the beautiful Caribbean island of Jamaica and immigrated with my family to the welcoming country of Canada, in May 1974. The last 40 years of my life have primarily been spent living in the City of Edmonton, Province of Alberta.

I graduated from Ross Sheppard High School in 1984, then attended the Business Administration Program at the Northern Alberta Institute of Technology, graduating with a diploma in Business Administration.

One of my major life accomplishments was becoming a member of the City of Edmonton Police Service (EPS). Through my 14 year tenure with EPS, I gained valuable life lessons which I have incorporated into my life's journey.

Writing was never on the horizon for me, but after leaving EPS I started to search for my purpose in life. During those times of searching, I would often pray and my thoughts flooded with words in the form of poetry. My prayer is that this collection of poems will be a Blessing to everyone who reads them and that they too will find their purpose in life.

The sole purpose for the remainder of my life is to bring the Good News of Salvation to everyone I encounter in my daily walk.

CPSIA information can be obtained
at www.ICGtesting.com
Printed in the USA
BVHW032303140321
602531BV00023B/342